*Party Games and Activities
for all Occasions, its....*

Organised Chaos

by Brian Thurston

Illustrated by Henry Dean

Cover design and illustration by Ron Branagan

Thurston, Brian
   Party games and activities for all
   occasions, - organised chaos.
   1. Children's parties. 2. Games
   I. Title
   793.2'1   GV1203

   ISBN 0-948834-40-4

Foreword

My aim is for YOU to enjoy the PARTY which you are hosting and if your guests are enjoying themselves you have reason to be happy. My games are mostly physical. They encourage people to mix and many are suitable for different age groups to play together.

The route from the SOFTLY-SOFTLY opening to CHAOS ACHIEVED is not a difficult trail to follow but you should remain flexible and do not be "pushy". Five or six games are usually enough for one party. Behind your carefree and enthusiastic presentation there should be serious forethought and careful planning.

I should like to thank my eldest daughter Jennifer for her consistent support, and Jack Gardiner who recklessly let me loose on the unsuspecting public at the Exmouth Pavilion ten years ago. Especially "thank you" to all those holiday families who played my silly games.

Brian Thurston

PRINTFORCE

6 Angel Hill Drive
Sutton
Surrey SM1 3BX

C O N T E N T S

Softly Softly

There are two consistent features of the games in the SOFTLY SOFTLY section. All take part together and no member makes a complete fool of themselves. This is the first step to gaining the confidence of the company. As the leading party organiser in the area, you are single minded in your determination to achieve three aims.

Firstly, no player must leave your party unhappy. This goal can be reached without the necessity of older children, or the adults, spending the evening in the kitchen devouring your food and drink, or the Pack practicing their knots on the tea towels.

Secondly, to live up to your reputation, you have no choice but to provide new experiences for each one. Something to be talked about for weeks ahead. "I don't know what got into me last night ... I was hopping around the floor pretending to be a Prince-turned-frog ... chasing Princess Di ... I won the game!"

Thirdly, and not the least important, you have to finish the evening overwhelmed by an agreeable degree of self-satisfaction!

Whispers

Players find their matching companions but are only allowed to do so by whispering to each other. A SUCCESSFUL MATCH IS THREE PLAYERS. The degree of difficulty is determined by the ages of the players.

Commence by giving a secret IDENTITY to each player. For the younger group the IDENTITIES could be KNIFE, FORK, SPOON, PLATE, SAUCER, CUP, BUCKET, SPADE, BEACH, EYES, NOSE, LIPS, DOG, BITCH, PUPPY etc.

When three believe they are a correct match, they tell you, again in a whisper, their identity. If wrong, you may confide the one that is out of place and all three remain in the contest. If correct, they win. The game continues until all correct groups are together.

The IDENTITIES you select relate to the age groups. Over nines may require references to the less obvious, whilst the twelve to fourteens could ponder over the intricacies of pop groups, television and computers. It is a rare opportunity to lean toward the educational pastime and, for example, geographical links are easily introduced using COUNTRIES, CAPITALS and CURRENCIES.

Fifteen year olds and beyond expect no charity from you! Make the IDENTITY connections obscure or IMPOSSIBLE if you wish. As an alternative, have only TWO GROUPS from the entire company.

Commercial Break

Perhaps you are familiar with the contest that requires participants to list the products of a series of advertisements which have been put on display. All clues have been removed from the pictures. COMMERCIAL BREAK requires neither pencil nor paper and although not boisterous, it does get everyone on their feet and active.

Label one corner of the hall as HONEST and one as DISHONEST. Hold an advertisement aloft and make a declaration. For example, I have a picture of a RUGBY FOOTBALL on a bed of GRASS, to which I could comment "This picture is an advertisement for metal racks and shelving. If I'm telling the truth go to the honest corner, but if I'm not telling the truth, go to the dishonest corner."

All choosing the wrong corner are eliminated and, using your next picture, another statement is made.

There is a limitless supply of material, particularly in weekend newspaper supplements.

It is suitable for all ages and the necessary adjustments are made both by the choice of pictures and the manner in which your statements are made. In using this with a mixed age group, I find the younger ones often win.

"All right, I'll put you out of your misery. Those that went to the HONEST CORNER for the RUGBY FOOTBALL poser, remain in the game. The rest drop out. As if I'd tell a lie!"

Food Themes for Younger Children

Zoo Party

Zebra bars   Fingers of pizza with alternating light and dark topping.

Monkey puzzles   Sausages with cheese pastry twisted in a spiral round.

Crocodile teeth   Thin cheese and carrot slices cut in triangles.

Porcupine spikes   Fruit, salad etc. on cocktail sticks stuck into a fruit or vegetable base.

Animal cheese biscuits placed around the dishes and small farmyard type toys placed generously about the table.

Space Theme

Moon, star, rocket shaped items.   Spaceburgers!

Moon buns   Large, soft baps with grilled cheese, tomato and bacon topping.

Planets   Nut covered cheese balls with a ring of tomato around.

Rockets   Rolled sandwiches - cheese slices for fins.

A Knotty Problem

I confess to not having tried this with very young children, but it does cause some merriment with older children and adults. No less than ten and perhaps no more than twenty may take part and begin by forming a circle, facing the centre.

All shuffle to the centre with their eyes closed and their hands outstretched, both upward and forward. Each hand should grasp an available free hand until everyone has their hands full!

The group may now open their eyes. The knot is complete. The objective is to untangle the knot but all hands must remain clasped until this is achieved.

An Open and Shut Case

Everyone may take part in this and they may be standing, seated, or either. Players should make a circle, a square, a triangle, a rectangle or any remote shape which produces an unbroken chain. The only prop is a case.

It could be either : a SPECTACLE case, a BRIEF case, SUIT case or any other case ... but it must OPEN and SHUT easily and shouldn't be too large if your party is for small people. The game begins with the CASE in YOUR hand. You have read the instructions! Open it and pass it to the person on your left and say "This is for you and it's OPEN."

The recipient must decide whether to pass the case to the next player OPEN or SHUT and as he does this he makes the appropriate comment, either:

"THIS IS FOR YOU AND IT'S OPEN" or
"THIS IS FOR YOU AND IT'S SHUT"

THE SECRET IS WITH THE FREE HAND. If it is holding an object i.e. a handkerchief, glass or someone elses hand, it is SHUT. It is also SHUT if it is clenched. THE DEFINITION OF "CLENCHED" BEING THE FINGERS WRAPPED AROUND THE THUMB. Should anyone pass the case with both hands, this is considered to be SHUT. With nothing in the free hand and the thumb free from the fingers, it is OPEN. Those who declare they have discovered the secret MUST NOT DIVULGE IT, but prove it by continually passing the case correctly.

The game ends when everyone is correct or when it becomes apparent some will never work it out!

The Warm Up

The Warm-Up is a little more physical, though
not a lot. It is certainly noisier but of course
you were never under the mis-apprehension a quiet
evening was on offer - were you?

Spin the Plate

Nothing new about this physical fracas. It is suitable for all ages and should also be tried with parents and children together.

Players should either sit or kneel in a circle. One stands in the centre and spins a plate on the floor. At the same time he calls out the name of one of the others who has to catch the plate before it stops spinning. As soon as the spinning commences, the spinner returns to his seat.

The person whose name was called, whether the plate was successfully caught or not, becomes the next spinner.

Each player has THREE lives.

Variations may include exchanging names. Each player has the name of the person immediately on the left and this is extended further by moving all names around one position between each spin.

Instead of losing a "life", a forfeit could be an option that allows a player to remain in the game.

DOUBLES is exhausting. However, if you insist, have light-weights as the "JOCKEYS". This version requires one member to be on all fours and the partner sitting on his back. The plate must be caught by the jockey without falling from the horse.

Shopping Spree

"I went to the shops and I bought a TOY CAR" says Sam. "I went to the shops and I bought a TOY CAR and a PAIR OF TIGHTS" adds Margaret.

John : "I went to the shops and I bought a TOY CAR, A PAIR OF TIGHTS and a HUTCH FOR MY RABBIT."

Jenny : "I went to the shops and I bought a TOY CAR, A PAIR OF TIGHTS, A HUTCH FOR MY RABBIT AND 1000 SHARES IN BRITISH GAS."

Simon : "I went to the shops and I bought a TOY CAR, A PAIR OF TIGHTS, A HUTCH FOR MY RABBIT, 1000 SHARES IN BRITISH GAS AND THE DAVID SAINT COLLECTION OF BOOKS."

This continues, each "shopper" repeating the previous list, and adding a new "buy" at the end. Usually the list grows to double figures before errors are made. A mistake eliminates the player, although his purchases must still be remembered by the other players.

Wicked but Wonderful

Four to six children each have a sticky jam dough-
nut and attempt to eat it without licking their
lips. The winner is the child with the least
number of "licks".

Each has a volunteer "counter" sitting opposite.

Sweet Unwrap

This is a little altered version of PASS THE PARCEL.
For those who have led a sheltered existence,
the essential ingredients are a multi-wrapped
parcel, music and a circle of eager children.

The centre of the parcel contains a box of sweets.
Each layer of wrapping holds a single sweet. The
music begins and the parcel is passed around the
circle. When the music stops, the player holding
the parcel must remove as many layers of paper
as possible before the music re-commences.

All layers of paper, and there shouldn't be less
than twenty, are tied loosely with string or with
a little adhesive tape. Please don't make the
unwrapping too difficult for the small children.

Up and Down

A piece of stout but not rough string of considerable length is required. Several pieces
can be tied together if necessary and it's threaded
through a variety of objects - one for each two
metres. Guests form a circle and it is better
for the positions to be alternatively male and
female and/or adult and child.

The aim is to completely thread the circle together
by taking the string down through the clothing
of one person and up through the clothing of the
next. Both ends of the string may begin simultaneously, one setting off to the left and one
to the right.

The bits and pieces on the string are at your
discretion. If no one is wearing jeans the largest
could be a toilet roll. Items might include a
bolt, button, washer, ring, spoon, toy spider,
wrist watch, woggle, and there are always objects
that could have a hole pre-drilled as, for example,
a carrot, a set of false teeth or orange peel.

**The lunatic fringe have been known to include
a knotted balloon with a drop of water inside.**

All having followed instructions successfully,
two bewildered participants, side by side, should
be holding an end of string. Tie the ends together.

Cut the string in two places to equally divide
the players into two teams, who must now compete
against each other to be the first to remove all
the objects but leave the string in place!

Bunkered

This stupendous step to stupidity surprisingly demands a high level of skill and concentration but with dozens of players crawling around the floor, the first is unlikely and the second impossible. Winning is often more by luck than judgement and cheating is not unknown! I shall be deeply offended if any reader avoids taking part.

Putting your famed fertile imagination to work, prepare an indoor golf course - it may be prudent not to include the area housing the food and drink. Coats, bodies, furniture, a bowl of shallow water, cats and dogs replace the conventional bunkers, trees and lakes too often found on a golf course.

The course may comprise several holes - the size of the premises determining the precise number. I suggest nine for a Church Hall, five for a Guide or Scout Hut, or forget all about it in a tent. The "holes" should be saucers or small bowls - not too small. Use pieces of cardboard to number the tees and the first "stroke" should be from immediately behind the cardboard.

A close scrutiny of scores is recommended if the winner is to receive a prize and scorecards could be used - they will not detract from the fun (may cause a few arguments) because - and here is the punchline - all your golfers are on their hands and knees with TIDDLY WINKS.

The "fairways" must be badly arranged, meeting and crossing at critical points, to ensure players frequently collide. "Twosomes" as an alternative to "singles" guarantee double collisions, double the cheating and double the scoring.

Seen in Print

Young teenagers will cope with this challenge with considerable aplomb but should work in pairs. Younger children will certainly need an adult, making the contest ideal for a family gathering.

Each child has a large and complete newspaper and a dozen pins. The parent has twenty minutes in which to make a fancy dress from the newspaper and pins. Many of the end results will be original and clever.

Select five judges who do not have their own children in the contest and give each a set of five cards marked from 6 to 10. Unknown to the competitors, the lowest mark is 6. Speak to each of the children and encourage applause for each one, then return to the beginning for the judging.

The judges now hold their cards aloft for competitor number 1. The total score is recorded and it is the turn of number 2.

Whilst it would not be necessary to go through this routine with older children, it is preferable with the younger set, one or two of whom may not respond too well if judgement is on applause, and they don't happen to get any!

Normandy Loaf

Makes an 800g (2 lb) loaf

Oven temperature : Gas   Reg 7
                   Electric 425F or
                             220C

Ingredients :

200g lean bacon
1 small onion
100g polyunsaturated margarine
1 level tablespoon chopped parsley
1 egg
250ml skimmed milk
50g firm low fat or cheddar cheese
400g self raising flour (if possible, a mixture of white and wholemeal)

Method :

1.   Put the oven on. Grease an 800g loaf tin.

2.   Remove the rind from the bacon and chop into small pieces.

3.   Peel and chop the onion. Chop the parsley finely. Grate the cheese finely.

4.   Place the bacon and onion in a small saucepan and cook together for 3 minutes.

5.   Place the flour in a bowl. Add the margarine and rub together with the fingertips until like fine breadcrumbs.

6. Stir in the bacon, onion and parsley and half the cheese.

7. Beat the egg in a measuring jug and make up to 250ml with milk. Add to the dry ingredients and mix to a soft dough.

8. Press the dough into the loaf tin. Brush with milk and sprinkle with the remaining grated cheese.

9. Bake for about 1 hour until well risen and golden brown. Leave in the tin for 5 minutes and then turn onto a wire rack to cool.

10. Serve spread with soft margarine or cream cheese, and salad.

In Full Swing

This is the point of no return.   The half-way stage.

Certain games from IN FULL SWING may test hitherto
unchallenged friendships, burst the ear drums,
bruise the bottom or strain the loin.

They will not, at any time, stretch the intelli-
gence!

Musical Hats

The aim of this piece of hilarity is not to be caught with a hat on the head when the music stops. Partners cling closely to each other whilst holding between them, at waist level, a ball or some other suitable object, which is kept in place **purely by the pressure.** It must not be touched by the hands.

Couples dance to the music and at the same time have to avoid a hat being placed on their heads by one of the other couples. If more than twenty pairs are dancing, there ought to be at least two hats circulating. Otherwise one hat is sufficient.

This does get somewhat hectic and apart from the "disc jockey", two assistants are necessary to dash about **amidst the confusion** collecting the dropped balls and eliminating couples if they prevent the hat being placed on their heads, touch the ball with their hands, drop it on the floor or have the hat when the music stops.

As the couples become fewer, some method of decreasing the floor area is necessary. This may be achieved by using chairs or other dancers as boundaries.

The exhausted assistants are also thieving magpies. On behalf of the very small children **they cheat quite openly,** relieving the young 'uns of the hat and chasing the older dancers with it.

The organiser invariably laughs uncontrollably and contributes little, if anything, to the organisation.

Musical Laps

At a family gathering with children aged ten years and under, this game HAS TO BE PLAYED. It encourages parents and children to take part together and if you are intending to be **devious** with the **rules of games,** this is the opportunity to be openly honest and thus gain the trust and confidence of everyone.

Parents sit on the floor in a circle, facing outwards, and the children walk around the outside of the circle to music. When the music stops the children sit (**flop, dive, fall**) on to the first available lap. Those who do not find a lap are eliminated.

Before the music starts again, a lap is removed. If there are hundreds of children, then remove several laps simultaneously.

Parental laps must make a contribution to the law and order of the party - **chaos shortly but not now** - by making an occasional decision when several children are attracted to the same lap.

Happy days!

Food Themes

Picnic Boxes

Cake boxes are available from bakers - each child has own box.

Individual pizza slices
Cheese filled celery
Savoury puffs (choux pastry/tuna)
Cocktail sticks with a variety of fruit,
salad items
Pigs in blankets (sausages with square
of cheese pastry wrapped around)

Sea Theme

Green shallow jelly with a fleet of plastic boats,
one for each child as a centre piece.

Savoury boats (pastry filled with savoury mixture,
cocktail stick with cucumber sail).

Out Out You Rascal

A piece of treasure, small in size, is wrapped in many layers of paper and each layer sealed or tied with string or wool. **Similar to SWEET UNWRAP and PASS THE PARCEL.** The other props are a very large dice, a kitchen chair, a large hat and a large pair of gloves.

The children sit on the floor in a semi-circle and take it in turns throwing the dice. A "6" is the key to the castle and the thrower gets into the castle by the castle gate - crawling under the chair - and then puts on the hat and the gloves and unwraps the parcel.

Whilst the castle is occupied by the intruder, the other children continue to throw the dice.

As soon as another "6" is thrown, all the children shout **"Out, out you rascal"** and the rascal must drop the treasure immediately, remove the hat and gloves and get back to the semi-circle before the new rascal arrives.

The reason for a semi-circle formation is to enable you to place a "retriever" at the open side of the circle to collect the dice and give it to the next player.

Bump and Pump

This piece of nonsense requires, in accord with most of my games, the participants to be told at the last possible moment of their impending embarrassment.

As a spectacle it is funnier with teenage children or parents BUMPING AND PUMPING than with the younger children. **Nevertheless, it is for any age over five.**

Four to six rubber or plastic footpumps are needed (used for pumping rubber dinghies, with a half metre tube attached). To the end of each tube is secured, with adhesive tape, a large and strong balloon.

Give the impression to the BUMPERS they are going to use the footpump in a conventional manner to inflate the balloons in a race to see who is able to burst their's first. At the last moment the pumps are placed on the chairs and each BUMPER sits on the footpump with the PIPE AND BALLOON protruding.

You've guessed. I really must say how impressed I am to discover that intelligent readers, such as yourself, are studying my book. The PUMPING is achieved by BUMPING the bottom (...backside... posterior...etc.) up and down on the footpump. To ensure the complete deflation of your barmy bouncers, you could use one or both of the following "extras". Use sausage shaped balloons and secretly put several pinpricks in the ends. Thus, the escaping air prolongs the agony and some wilting will be evident. Whenever you give the command they must leap up from the chair, run and touch the far wall and return to the footpump.

Cops and Robbers

A near perfect opportunity for children and parents to participate together. Six adult and child partnerships are a comfortable maximum, although having found the volunteers, you immediately divide into two teams, one of adults and one of children.

A large floor area is essential and the children taking part should not be over ten years of age.

One adult is selected to be the ROBBER and two children to be the COPS. All three are blindfolded. The ROBBER is placed in the centre of the arena and a COP is placed at each end. All three must crawl on their hands and knees and if expense is no problem, the players can be dressed for their roles.

The other team members are spread around the room and give commands to their colleagues (**ear plugs for onlookers**). When instructions are spoken, shouted or screamed by the COPS team, there are no restrictions. The ROBBERS team, however, may only use four commands : "backward", "forward", "left" and "right" - a minor snag being that each command must mean the opposite or should be in a foreign language.

Foreign alternatives :

	Left	Right	Backward	Forward
Dutch	Links	Rechts	Achteruit	Vooruit
French	Gauche	Droit	A reculons	Avant
Double	Links	Rechts	Achteruit	Vooruit
Dutch	Links	Rechts	Achteruit	Vooruit

Fetch Me

If you've arrived at this page and are hoping to find a sophisticated and quiet attempt from the writer to allow your gathering to recover, you have completely and utterly failed to grasp the lunatic objectives of this manual. However, FETCH ME does have one attribute. It is controllable!

FETCH ME is basically for the children aged five to eleven when in the company of their parents. With a generous mound of sweets on hand, you announce you have three sweets for the first child to "FETCH ME" certain items - FETCH ME a man's belt - a set of black teeth - a leek - a wooden cigarette lighter - a nursery rhyme - three socks - an empty ladies handbag - a pretty mother - an ugly dad - FETCH ME a dad with a mum's hands in his trouser pockets - something no one else has - a man's shirt - 4 pairs of Guides' socks and 4 pairs of Scouts' socks tied together in a sheepshank etc.

Penultimate Chaos

THIS IS THE STAGE AT WHICH,
AS YOU PHYSICALLY TAKE PART IN THE PROCEEDINGS,
YOU BEGIN TO BELIEVE YOU HAVE SUNK
TO THE ULTIMATE DEPTH OF
NONSENSICAL ACTIVITY AND SANITY.

YOU'RE QUITE WRONG - OF COURSE.

THERE IS ANOTHER CHAPTER AFTER THIS ONE!

Chaoticards

Shuffle two or three packs of playing cards together and deal them to all players, who then place their cards upon the top of their heads. This group of oddballs remain in a circle facing the centre, which should be occupied by someone with a warped sense of humour - YOU HAVE JUST VOLUNTEERED! - from whom instructions shall come forth.

The winner of the game is the player who collects all the cards.

1. Give all players a fictitious name which they must be able to pronounce. The very young players could have names of characters from their favourite books or from nursery rhymes. For example : Goldilocks, Rupert, Winnie the Pooh, Humpty Dumpty, Miss Muffet etc., whilst a group of older children may have place names such as : Albuquerque, Abruzzi-e-Molise, Schaumburg-Lipp, Zvenigoroodka, Megalokastron, Milton Keynes etc., - **each having an air of mystery about it** - and bid the entire circle to state their names one at a time to allow everyone a chance to learn all the names. (**Quite impossible, of course.**)

2. When cards fall from a player's head, **upon which they rest without any other aid,** the first person to shout the player's name collects all but one of the cards that have fallen. The collector must get the cards, **without touching or dropping his own cards.** Should anyone have only one card and it drops, this is the elimination for which he or she may be thankful!

3. Your contribution to this is vital for without you there is a real fear that one or two players may retain their composure and become serious about winning. You must shout the orders! "Everyone ready - lift your right foot off the floor - raise your left arm - return to ready - turn a complete circle - go down on your knees - stand up - shake hands with the player either side of you - take off your shoes for starters(?)" and whilst all this is happening, a fierce argument is raging over whether or not The Valley of Winds spat out Oraefajokull correctly.

Sorry - Custard Pie Foam

Best you know at the outset what you are letting yourself in for, or in to!

The dreaded concoction is available at novelty shops and some toy shops. Cardboard plates are needed.

Five couples are ample for this. With older children (perhaps 13+) select boys and girls who know each other well and it is the boy who eventually suffers. It can also be played with parent and child pairs and in this event - **you are right again** - it is the parent who is on the receiving end of the CUSTARD PIE. The "SORRY" is mentioned at this stage in a naive attempt to placate the parent.

Take the five girls (teenage party) or the five children (family) into another room and ask each of them four questions concerning their likes and dislikes, or the habits of their trusting partner. List these and return to the battlefield.

The victims sit in a row with their partner standing behind armed with the CUSTARD PIE.

Ask each of the seated victims the questions. Should they not answer correctly, one face meets one pie, courtesy of the overjoyed partner. Actually, all five pies find their target, because even if they answer all the questions correctly, you LIE about the last answer.

Recipe

Pizza (scone based)   Makes 16 fingers

Oven temperature : Gas Reg 8
                   Electric 425F or 220C

Ingredients :

200g self raising flour (a mixture of white and
wholemeal if possible)
75g polyunsaturated margarine
200ml skimmed milk

Toppings : **Choose from** :

Sardine & Tomato : Can of tomatoes with the
juice drained off or 300g peeled sliced tomatoes
2 cans of sardines in tomato sauce

Tomato : Can tomatoes with the juice drained
off or 300g peeled sliced tomatoes
1 onion - peeled and chopped
1 desertspoon basil or marjoram
Cook these ingredients together in a saucepan
until the onion is soft

Vegetable : 50g mushrooms - washed and chopped
200g tomatoes - peeled and sliced
100g sweetcorn, drained
50g grated cheese

Ham and sweetcorn : 75g ham - chopped
Small can sweetcorn - drained
250ml milk, 25g wholemeal flour, 25g margarine
(made into roux sauce)
25g cheese - grated and stirred into the sauce

Method :

1. Put the oven on. Grease a 30cm x 18cm swiss roll tin.

2. Prepare the topping as overleaf.

3. Put the flour into a mixing bowl. Rub in the fat until like fine breadcrumbs.

4. Add enough milk to make a soft (scone) dough.

5. Roll out to fit the tin.

6. Place the pizza in the tin, pressing well into the corners.

7. Cover with the prepared topping.

8. Bake for 30 minutes until golden brown and firm. Remove to a wire rack and allow to cool.

9. When cold, cut into 16 fingers and wrap in silver foil.

Fill the Bottle

You don't want to get your floor wet? Then why not take your party into the garden?

Two buckets of water. Two empty milk bottles. Eight shallow saucers. Two teams of lunatics. One ample garden. Long suffering neighbours. You're ready!

A team stands one behind each other with the bucket of water at the front and the empty bottle at the back. The first team to fill the bottle with water from their bucket is declared the winner. The water is transferred from the bucket to the bottle, using only the four saucers, and these must be passed under the legs of the entire team. The saucers, having been emptied into the bottle, are returned via the same route to the front team member.

"I shall now present the winners with their prize" you announce "will eight members of the winning team each bring me a saucer and I'll put something special in it." At this stage, have a cardboard box on hand to suggest you really do have prizes.

The eight have each to balance the saucer on their heads. Water is poured into each saucer, some considerable spillage of course, and the REAL COM-PETITION begins. This is a race to the bottom of the garden and back. From the first four to cross the line, the winner is the player with the most water remaining in the saucer. Do not labour under the mis-apprehension that you, as organiser, have special protection or immunity during such foolish games. You will, I assure you, finish with the remainder of the buckets of water - over your head. A promise, not a threat!

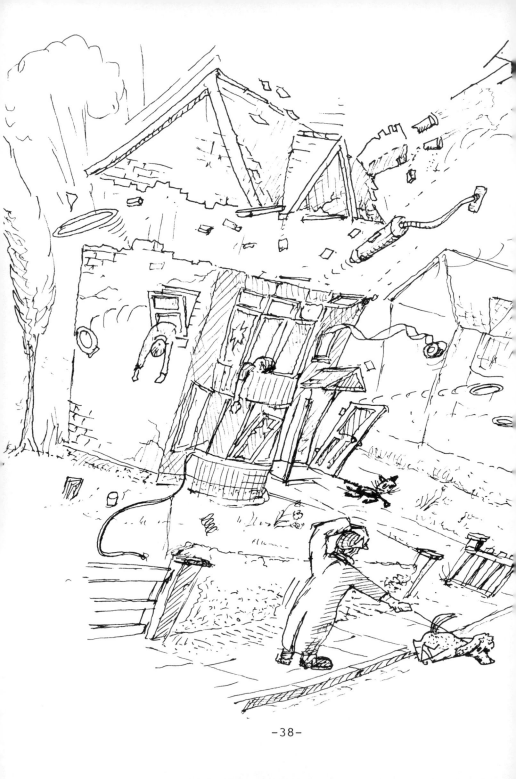

Chaos Achieved

To control or not to control, that is the question!
Chaos or ORGANISED CHAOS?

Having brought the party to a critical stage, you
have to hang on in there and channel the exuberance
rather than sit back and allow it to develop itself.
They'll always be a few "cheeky rascals" around,
aged between 6 and 106.

It is often the case that the hosts believe they
know exactly what is happening at a party, but
discover far more when clearing up afterwards.
This doesn't only apply to parties for children
that have reached their teens!

Chaos 1

There are no age qualifications and anyone may take part who can read and write. It is a PAIRS contest.

The READER has a page from a newspaper and the partner has a sheet of plain paper, a pencil and clip-board. The writer, quite simply, must get down on paper everything the READER shouts during a pre-determined period of time.

Each READER stands opposite each partner WRITER. The space between is considerable, i.e. the length of the room if indoors or, if outside, use the neighbours' garden as well as your own.

The greater the number taking part, the greater the possibility that no WRITER will get more than one correct word on paper!

The winners are the pair whose written offering is closest to its printed original. It leaves the judges with the task of placing some value on various shades of vagueness! Occasionally, with more luck than judgement, a few words are strung together successfully. Such initiatives should be treated with disdain. It is outrageous to go to all this trouble planning ridiculous games if someone insists on showing off!

If pairs are parent and child combinations, the parent takes the WRITER'S part. At the end each writer should read the result aloud whilst YOU, having consulted the READER, check against the newspaper report and use the opportunity to make fun of their efforts.

This is noisy!

The noise level is parallel to CHAOS 1. Not true; it is far worse. Close to unbearable!

To this bedlam we now add movement, blindfolds and an assortment of objects. CHAOS was not a description lightly chosen.

The same positional arrangement applies to CHAOS 2. Partners face each other from a considerable distance - for a short while - and if parents and children are together, the child is going to shout the instructions and the parent is to seek the treasure.

Each partnership is given an object which, you suggest to them, they'll recognise in the dark. I use a - set of false teeth - hoop - wig - feather duster - grass skirt - toilet roll - toilet seat - puppet - balloon - false nose and an outsize pair of sunglasses.

Rules are introduced at this stage! The SEEKERS are to be blindfolded and must find their particular piece of dubious treasure relying only on the instructions given, shrieked, screamed by their partners, who must remain seated throughout.

Speed is essential when hiding the treasure. As soon as the blindfolds are in place - I have two assistants helping with this - YOU (can you really cope with all this responsibility?) literally grab an innocent bystander and heap all the rubbish onto him or her. At the same time you must completely mis-lead the seekers by offering a running commentary : "This can go over here - this under here - the duster on top of this - what about something over the other side - ahh yes, the false nose."

The human treasure chest should wear the grass skirt, the nose and wig etc., and may move around for half a minute avoiding any TREASURE SEEKER who may get close by mistake. It would have to be a mistake for the din is quite deafening and instructions are impossible to hear. It is amusing to watch. I have never dared to ask anyone if they enjoyed playing!

I don't have to explain who the winner is, do I?

Anticipating your groans of dis-belief when you read CHAOS 3 I am duty bound, if only to protect the book from being torn apart, to ASSURE YOU THIS GAME IS PLAYABLE and people have been known to play a second time (although admittedly with a **twelve** month break).

Set up CHAOS 1. The newspapers, pencils, boards and the pairs opposite each other at the NORTH and SOUTH ends of the room.

Set up CHAOS 2. The objects, the blindfolds and the pairs opposite each other at the WEST AND EAST ends of the room.

Play both games simultaneously - IF YOU DARE!

GO!!

Food Themes

French Theme

Red and white checked cloth

French bread

Pate

Cheese

Normandy loaf

Salads

Grapes

Wine for adults

Fruit punch for children

French flags, ribbon - free from Food & Wine from France

A beret for George

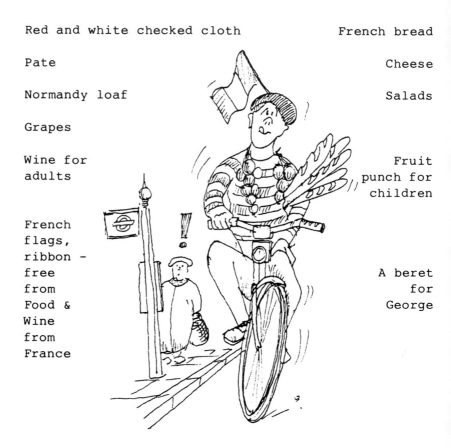

A Piaf record for Diana and Bert

A bicycle and onions for the Skipper

Recipe - Monkey Puzzles

Oven temperature : Gas   Reg 6   Makes 16
Electric 400F or
200C

Ingredients :

16 low fat thin sausages   50g plain white flour
50g plain wholemeal flour   Cold water to mix
50g polyunsaturated margarine
1 tablespoon tomato sauce
1 tablespoon brown sauce

Method :

1. Put the oven on. Grease a baking tray.

2. Prick the sausages with a fork.

3. Make shortcrust pastry by rubbing the fat into the flour with finger tips until like fine breadcrumbs. Add enough water to make a stiff dough.

4. Turn the pastry dough onto a lightly floured board and knead lightly.

5. Roll pastry to a 22cm square. Cut the square in half. Spread one half with tomato sauce and the other half with brown sauce.

6. Cut each half into 8 strips. Wrap one strip, sauce covered side inwards, around each sausage in a spiral.

7. Place on the baking tray.

8. Bake 30 minutes until the sausages are cooked and the pastry golden brown.

9. Remove from the baking tray onto a wire rack. Serve cold.

Flying Yolk

Although I have staged this at the Exmouth Pavilion for seven years, it does need a good deal of preparation to protect the walls, floor, furniture and the participants. The title provides the clue.

To save the trouble of covering everything with polythene and paper, play this in the garden. A large open air space - passers-by may show their interest by telephoning the funny farm - is optional.

Begin by asking for volunteers who can catch. It is a pairs contest and only one of each pair need be adept at this ancient skill. Hold a table-tennis ball in the air. Throw it to one or two likely victims. If they catch it, congratulate them on qualifying! The egg is only introduced when the first couple are in position and ready to throw.

Although this description applies to adult-child pairings, the game is suited to children over eight and to teenagers. The adult is the catcher and the child (boy or girl) is the thrower. The couple stand only 2 metres apart and nothing fragile or precious should be in the immediate vicinity of the parent (i.e. greenhouse, cat, Morris Traveller, double glazing or garden gnome).

The child throws the egg and the adult, in what transpires to be a successful attempt at catching the missile, sinks to her knees with hands in a praying posture. **Purely coincidental.** THE CHILD THEN GOES TO THE ADULT AND COLLECTS THE EGG **because** the child may **drop a thrown return** and your aim is to have the children laughing at the adults' expense.

This stupidity continues. Each time the child throws from a further distance, until on the sixth attempt MUM leaps at a wild overhead throw (remembering her NETBALL days), crushes the egg - some UGHH avoids the protective clothing and gets in her hair and down her neck - whilst a further YUK continues at right-angles, coming to rest on the latest releases carefully selected and paid for by the disc jockey earlier in the day.

The winners are the couple making the most number of catches. The Exmouth record, set up in 1982, is 34.